WORLD LINK 2

DEVELOPING ENGLISH FLUENCY

FOURTH EDITION

WORKBOOK

Australia · Brazil · Canada · Mexico · Singapore · United Kingdom · United States

National Geographic Learning,
a Cengage Company

World Link Level 2 Workbook
Fourth Edition

Publisher: Sherrise Roehr

Executive Editor: Sarah Kenney

Development Editor: Adam Robinson

Director of Global Marketing: Ian Martin

Heads of Regional Marketing:
Charlotte Ellis (Europe, Middle East and Africa)
Irina Pereyra (Latin America)

Senior Product Marketing Manager: Caitlin Thomas

Content Project Manager: Beth Houston

Media Researcher: Stephanie Eenigenburg

Cover/Text Design: Lisa Trager

Art Director: Brenda Carmichael

Operations Support: Hayley Chwazik-Gee, Avi Mednick

Manufacturing Planner: Mary Beth Hennebury

Composition: MPS North America LLC

ISBN: 978-0-357-50386-7

National Geographic Learning
5191 Natorp Boulevard
Mason, OH, 45040
USA

Locate your local office at **international.cengage.com/region**

Visit National Geographic Learning online at **ELTNGL.com**
Visit our corporate website at **www.cengage.com**

Printed in the United States of America
Print Number: 02 Print Year: 2023

TABLE OF CONTENTS

PHOTO CREDITS

Illustrations: All illustrations are owned by © Cengage.

6 Brian A. Witkin/Shutterstock.com; **8** (cl1) Iurii Kachkovskyi/Shutterstock.com, (cl2) eli_asenova/E+/Getty Images, (cr1) dja65/iStock/Getty Images, (cr2) vicm/iStock/Getty Images, (bl) Lew Robertson/Stone/Getty Images, (br) Image Source/Corbis; **13** 4kodiak/iStock/Getty Images; **16** tolstnev/iStock/Getty Images; **17** Everett Collection/ Shutterstock.com; **36** (tl) (tc) RichVintage/E+/Getty Images, (tr) kali9/iStock/Getty Images; **42** Erika Goldring/Getty Images Entertainment/Getty Images; **43** Lisa S/Shutterstock.com; **48** Onur Ersin/Shutterstock.com; **54** SpeedKingz/ Shutterstock.com; **55** sculpies/Shutterstock.com; **66** RossHelen/Shutterstock.com.

1 MY LIFE

A PEOPLE

VOCABULARY

A Write definitions for the words and phrases.

1. colleague *someone you work with*
2. classmate ______________
3. get along well ______________
4. going out ______________
5. neighbor ______________
6. next-door neighbor ______________
7. old friend ______________
8. girlfriend ______________
9. close friend ______________

B Complete the sentences with the words and phrases in the box.

classmate	colleague	get along well	going out	next-door
close	friend	girlfriend	neighbor	old

1. My ______________ and I have been ______________ for five months.
2. Her ______________ always asks a lot of questions in meetings.
3. He is with his ______________ in the library working on a presentation.
4. Our new ______________ plays very loud music. We can hear it from across the street.
5. I don't ______________ with my older sister, but my younger brother and I are very ______________.
6. I'm meeting an ______________ ______________ from high school who I haven't seen in 15 years.
7. She shares Wi-Fi with her ______________ neighbor.

C Who are they? Complete the chart with the names of people in your life.

Coworkers / classmates	
Neighbors	
Old friends	
Family members I get along with	

CONVERSATION

A Unscramble the words to make sentences.

1. to / introduce / you / like / I'd / cousin / my / to

____

2. Andres, / Mr. Park / is / this

____

3. very / meet / to / nice / you, / Salma / it's

____

4. sorry, / terrible / names / with / I'm

____

5. Mom, / meet / like / you / Daniel / to / I'd

____

6. I've / sorry, / forgotten / I'm / name / your

____

B Number the sentences in order to make a conversation.

_____ I'm good! And you?

_____ Hi, Emily.

_____ Busy, but good. Oh, and this is my mom. She's visiting this weekend.

_____ Hi, Yuna! How are you?

_____ It's really nice to meet you, too.

_____ Hello, Mrs. Kim! Nice to meet you!

C Write conversations.

1. Introduce your best friend to a new friend.

You: ______________________________

Best friend: ______________________________

New friend: ______________________________

2. Introduce a classmate to a member of your family.

You: ______________________________

Classmate: ______________________________

Family member: ______________________________

3. Introduce an old friend to a neighbor.

You: ______________________________

Old friend: ______________________________

Neighbor: ______________________________

GRAMMAR

A Richard is a teacher, but now he's on vacation. Look at the pictures and write sentences about him using the simple present or the present continuous.

Usually	Today
He ______________.	He ______________.
He ______________.	He ______________.
He ______________.	He ______________.
He ______________.	He ______________.

B Complete each sentence with the correct form of the verb in parentheses. Use the simple present or the present continuous.

1. Sorry, I can't talk to you right now. I ______________ (be) late for work.
2. Felipe ______________ (not, like) loud music.
3. Don't turn off the TV! I ______________ (watch) a great movie.
4. Sarah usually ______________ (play) tennis with her friends on Saturday.
5. I ______________ (study) English now. I ______________ (study) every day for an hour after class.
6. This basketball game is really exciting—my team ______________ (win) by only two points!
7. Usually, my mother ______________ (cook) dinner, but today my brother ______________ (cook) for us.
8. Pierre ______________ (not, drink) coffee. He ______________ (like) tea.

C In your notebook, write four sentences about things you usually do and four sentences about things you are doing today. Use the simple present and the present continuous.

B LESSONS LEARNED

VOCABULARY AND GRAMMAR

A Match the sentence halves.

_____ 1. Which classes are	a. grades this time.
_____ 2. Studying is important,	b. but we can have fun, too.
_____ 3. The study group meets on	c. my final exams for months.
_____ 4. I've been preparing for	d. lessons after work.
_____ 5. She's taking guitar	e. you taking this year?
_____ 6. I hope to get good	f. Thursday afternoons in the library.
_____ 7. Did you	g. pass or fail?

B Complete the paragraph with the words in the box. Use the simple past.

be	find	finish	get	go	live	move	want

When Chang was young, his family **(1.)** _____________ in a small town. When he was eight, they **(2.)** _____________ to Shanghai. Chang **(3.)** _____________ a good education there. He **(4.)** _____________ to become a computer programmer. He **(5.)** _____________ college when he was 20 years old. Then he **(6.)** _____________ to New York City for a job interview. Chang **(7.)** _____________ very lucky, and he got the job. He also **(8.)** _____________ a cheap apartment, which was also very lucky. Chang invited his parents to visit him, but it was too far for them to travel.

C Read more about Chang's life. Underline the regular simple past verbs. Circle the irregular ones.

For many years, Chang worked very hard. Sometimes he forgot to eat lunch because he had so much work to do. He rarely slept because he stayed late at the office. He liked his job and he enjoyed going out with friends on the weekend, but he wondered what other jobs he could apply for. He also wanted to visit his family in China. One day, Chang saw a job posting online. A school needed an IT instructor. The school was in Shanghai! Chang did not know what to do. He had a big decision to make . . . .

READING AND WRITING

A Read the article.

Against all odds

Bethany Hamilton

Bethany Hamilton fell in love with surfing at a young age. She went surfing every day after school and even won competitions when she was only eight years old. Bethany felt peaceful and happy when she surfed, and it was a very important part of her life.

One day, when surfing, she was attacked by a shark. She survived the attack, but she lost her left arm. After such a terrible experience, many people would give up surfing and stay away from the water forever. But Bethany taught herself to surf with just one arm. She was surfing again after only one month! She even won a competition just three months after the attack.

Eric Yuan

Eric Yuan was born in China. When he was a young man, he traveled 10 hours to visit his girlfriend. This difficult journey made him think about how people communicate over long distances. After college, he tried to follow his dream of working in the US. He failed to get a visa to the US. eight times. But Yuan didn't give up.

He kept trying, and in 1997, he succeeded. He didn't speak any English when he arrived, but he studied hard and learned to speak well. After seven years in different jobs, he started his own company and called it Zoom.

Now, Zoom is a very successful technology company. It's used by millions of people every day. Eric even married the girlfriend he traveled for hours to see. He says those difficult journeys helped him become a success.

B Circle **T** for *true* or **F** for *false*.

1. Bethany Hamilton only surfed on the weekend. **T F**
2. Bethany Hamilton won competitions before she was 10. **T F**
3. Bethany Hamilton was attacked by a shark. **T F**
4. Bethany Hamilton stopped surfing for three months. **T F**
5. Eric Yuan drove for 10 hours to see his girlfriend. **T F**
6. Eric Yuan tried to get a visa eight times. **T F**
7. Eric Yuan started his company the year he arrived in the US. **T F**
8. Eric Yuan has a wife. **T F**

C Complete the paragraph. Use the simple past of the verbs in parentheses.

At the age of 13, I **(1.)** ______________ (travel) alone for the first time. I **(2.)** ______________ (go) to visit my grandparents in Los Angeles. I **(3.)** ______________ (feel) very nervous about traveling so far, but my mother **(4.)** ______________ (say), "Don't worry. You'll be fine." I **(5.)** ______________ (get) on the airplane and **(6.)** ______________ (talk) for a long time to a very nice woman who **(7.)** ______________ (sit) next to me. My grandparents **(8.)** ______________ (meet) me at the airport and **(9.)** ______________ (take) me to their home. I **(10.)** ______________ (stay) there for two weeks, and I **(11.)** ______________ (have) so much fun with them! It **(12.)** ______________ (be) my first time in Los Angeles, and I **(13.)** ______________ (see) lots of really interesting places. In the end, I **(14.)** ______________ (not, want) to go home!

D Write about somebody you know who didn't give up.

____

____

____

____

____

____

____

2

LET'S EAT!

A FOODS WE LIKE

VOCABULARY

A Unscramble the letters to write words that describe food.

1. yatst ___tasty___
2. ycpsi ______
3. ckdooe ______
4. tewes ______
5. dreif ______
6. sidecliuo ______
7. ijuyc ______
8. yoli ______
9. rosu ______
10. talys ______
11. zonefr ______
12. trebleri ______
13. muyym ______
14. kabed ______
15. lidm ______
16. flauw ______

B Label the photos with words from **A**. There may be more than one correct answer.

1. ______
2. ______
3. ______
4. ______
5. ______
6. ______

C Match the opposites. There may be more than one correct answer.

______ 1. sweet
______ 2. spicy
______ 3. tasty
______ 4. cooked
______ 5. delicious

a. awful
b. sour
c. juicy
d. terrible
e. mild
f. frozen

CONVERSATION

A Unscramble the words to make suggestions.

1. movie / a / how / tonight / going / to / about

   ______________________________?

2. ice cream / why / class / don't / we / after / have / some

   ______________________________?

3. have / let's / food / Brazilian / tonight

   ______________________________.

4. don't / meet / why / 8:00 / we / at

   ______________________________?

5. playing / how / tennis / tomorrow / about

   ______________________________?

B Number the sentences in order to make a conversation.

_____ You're right. I had fried food for lunch anyway.

_____ OK! Why don't we go to Carl's Chicken?

_____ Well, how about that salad place down the street?

_____ That's a great idea. Their food is much healthier.

_____ Would you like to go out for dinner tonight?

_____ I'm sorry, but I don't like their food. It's too oily.

C What would you like to do tonight? Write conversations between you and a friend and you and a family member.

1. **You:** *Would you . . .*

   Your friend: ______________________________

   You: ______________________________

   Your friend: ______________________________

   You: ______________________________

   Your friend: ______________________________

2. **Family member:** ______________________________

   You: ______________________________

   Family member: ______________________________

   You: ______________________________

   Family member: ______________________________

   You: ______________________________

GRAMMAR

A Write the comparative form of the adjectives.

1. cold ____________________
2. friendly ____________________
3. good ____________________
4. nice ____________________
5. hard ____________________
6. easy ____________________

B Write sentences with the comparative form of these adjectives. Use your own ideas.

1. phone calls / texts / nice *Phone calls are nicer than texts.*
2. cats / dogs / friendly ____________________
3. cooking / eating out / expensive ____________________
4. Mexico City / Tokyo / interesting ____________________
5. fried chicken / french fries / oily ____________________
6. cookies / donuts / sweet ____________________
7. cleaning the house / cooking / hard ____________________
8. sharks / snakes / dangerous ____________________
9. history class / math class / hard ____________________
10. (your idea) ____________________

C Complete the paragraph with the correct comparative form of the adjectives provided.

My mother is a great cook. She's **(1.)** ____________________ (good) at cooking than anyone in my family. The food she prepares is always **(2.)** ____________________ (tasty) than anything you can get at a restaurant. One of my favorite things she makes is baked chicken. It's **(3.)** ____________________ (juicy) than the chicken I make, and it's **(4.)** ____________________ (spicy) than you might expect! She also bakes a great chocolate cake. Her recipe is **(5.)** ____________________ (unusual) than one you would find in a cookbook. She puts coffee in the cake batter. But, don't worry! The cake is not bitter. It's **(6.)** ____________________ (sweet) and **(7.)** ____________________ (delicious) than anything from the bakery. I think my mom should open her own restaurant, but she thinks that's an even **(8.)** ____________________ (crazy) idea than putting coffee in a cake!

B EATING WELL

VOCABULARY AND GRAMMAR

A Match the sentence halves.

_____ 1. There are a lot of health
_____ 2. Eating too much
_____ 3. You should drink less coffee
_____ 4. I need healthier habits,
_____ 5. There are plenty of

a. like drinking more water.
b. vegetables in this soup.
c. sugar increases your blood pressure.
d. benefits to eating spinach.
e. to prevent having a bad night's sleep.

B Complete the sentences with the words in the box.

diets	health benefits	lifestyle	prevent
habits	increases	plenty	reduced

1. A study found that Spanish people have a very healthy __________.
2. I eat __________ of vegetables, but I need more fruit in my diet.
3. There are so many __________ to drinking green tea.
4. Eating fried food __________ the chance of having heart problems.
5. I __________ the amount of coffee I drink. I only have two cups per day now.
6. My doctor says eating dark green vegetables can help __________ illnesses.
7. She finds it difficult to change her unhealthy eating __________.
8. I've tried so many different __________, but I am not losing any weight!

C Write sentences with the superlative form of these adjectives.

1. exciting / sport in the Olympics
   I think that skiing is the most exciting sport in the Olympics.
2. interesting / place in our country
   ____
3. good / restaurant in my town
   ____
4. quiet / person I know
   ____
5. interesting / show on TV now
   ____
6. big / problem in the world today
   ____
7. bad / habit
   ____

READING AND WRITING

A Answer these questions.

1. What are some spicy foods? ______________________
2. Do you like any of these foods? ______________________
3. Which countries are famous for spicy food? ______________________
4. Do you think spicy food is good for your health? ______________________
   Why or why not? ______________________

B Read the article.

Hot, hotter, hottest! Surprising facts about chili peppers

(1.) Chili peppers are one of the oldest food **crops** in the world. Farmers grew the first chilies more than 9,000 years ago.

(2.) The first chili peppers probably grew in Bolivia. From there, the plant **spread** through South America and the Caribbean. Christopher Columbus brought the first chili peppers to Europe.

(3.) The heat in the chilies comes from a chemical called *capsaicin*. Capsaicin has no smell or flavor, but it makes your mouth feel "hot."

(4.) Scientists believe that chili peppers are a very healthy food because they **are rich in** vitamins. Research shows that chilies do not **damage** the stomach, and Indian scientists discovered that eating chilies can help people lose weight.

(5.) Indian food is **well known** for using lots of chili peppers, but Thai food is spicier. The average person in Thailand eats five grams of chili pepper every day—the most in the world!

(6.) The Aztecs of Mexico loved chili peppers so much that they gave them to their king as a gift.

(7.) One of the hottest chili peppers in the world is the habanero. It is bright orange and grows in the Caribbean.

(8.) There are chili sauce factories on every **continent** except Antarctica.

C Match the words from the reading with their meanings.

_____ 1. crop	a. hurt
_____ 2. spread	b. move over an area
_____ 3. are rich in	c. farm plant
_____ 4. damage	d. famous
_____ 5. well known	e. large land area
_____ 6. continent	f. have many

D Circle **T** for *true* or **F** for *false*. Write the number of the section where you found the answers.

1. Mexicans eat the most chili peppers in the world. **T** **F** ____
2. Chilies are "hot" because they have capsaicin in them. **T** **F** ____
3. You can find chili sauce factories in Antarctica. **T** **F** ____
4. The first chili peppers grew in Europe. **T** **F** ____
5. Thai food is spicier than Indian food. **T** **F** ____
6. Chili peppers can be dangerous for your health. **T** **F** ____

E Read the paragraph and circle the correct words.

I'm from Korea, and kimchi is the **(1.)** (famous / most famous) food from my country. It's made from vegetables, chili peppers, garlic, and salt. Its flavor is sour, salty, and **(2.)** (spicy / spicier). The **(3.)** (most popular / popularest) kind of kimchi is made from cabbage, but there are many other kinds. White kimchi doesn't have chili peppers, so it's **(4.)** (milder / the most mild) than others. The **(5.)** (more spicier / spiciest) kind of kimchi is made from radishes. Kimchi is **(6.)** (healthiest / healthier) than many other vegetable dishes because it has more vitamins. I love kimchi, and I eat it every day. Some people don't like it, but I think they should try some different kinds. In my opinion, cucumber kimchi is the **(7.)** (more delicious / most delicious).

F Write about a famous dish from your country. What is it made from? How does it taste? Do you like it? Why or why not? Do other people like it?

___

___

___

___

___

___

___

___

___

___

___

3

MYSTERIES

A YOU'RE IN LUCK!

VOCABULARY

A Match the words and phrases with the meanings.

__g__ 1. more likely to
____ 2. take a chance
____ 3. increase
____ 4. chances
____ 5. avoid
____ 6. on purpose
____ 7. bring good luck
____ 8. by chance

a. go up
b. make something good happen
c. do something without knowing the result
d. how likely something will happen
e. mean to (do something)
f. stay away from
g. will probably choose to do (something)
h. by accident

B Complete the sentences using the words and phrases from **A**.

1. My grandmother believes you are ____________ have bad luck if you break a mirror.
2. I met an old school friend ____________ in the street today. It was a nice surprise.
3. I want to ____________ the traffic. Let's go another way.
4. Did you upset him ____________ or was it an accident?
5. In Spain, we eat twelve grapes before midnight on New Year's Eve to ____________ in the new year.
6. If you study using this method, it will ____________ your ____________ of passing the test.
7. I don't want to buy tickets yet. I am going to ____________ that I can get them cheaper on the day of the concert.

C Answer the questions. Use your own ideas and the words in bold in your answers.

1. In the United States, it's **bad luck** to open an umbrella inside. What's bad luck in your country?
____
2. "No one is successful without some **good luck**." Do you agree or disagree? Why?
____
3. "People should only make decisions based on facts." Do you agree or disagree?
____

CONVERSATION

A Unscramble the words to make sentences.

1. that / I / goes / rock climbing / doubt / Javier

____.

2. your cousin / the party / organize / perhaps / will / us / help

____.

3. bet / the game / she / I / wins / that

____.

4. Muhammad / answer / probably / the / knows

____.

5. walks / maybe / he / to work

____.

B Number the sentences in order to make a conversation.

__1__ I just spoke to Anna.
_____ Oh right, I forgot. Maybe she is saving for a vacation.
_____ She's great. She saved so much money this summer.
_____ I'm not sure. Perhaps she wants to buy a new car.
_____ How is she?
_____ I doubt that. She just got hers last year.
_____ Why? Is she planning to buy something?
_____ Maybe she is. She always talks about visiting Vietnam again.

C In your notebook, write answers to the questions. Use expressions from **A** and **B** in Vocabulary.

1. Do you think there is life on other planets?
2. Do you think your country will win 10 gold medals in the next Olympics?
3. Do you think you will travel to another continent this year?

GRAMMAR

A Circle the stative verbs in this paragraph.

I love to camp! It's my favorite way to spend my vacation. Every year, my family and I camp in a national park. We sleep in a tent and hike every day. I like to cook over a fire, and the food always tastes wonderful. For a whole week, I see lovely scenery and smell fresh air. At night, I hear the wind blow in the trees, and I feel so peaceful. It doesn't cost much to camp, and I believe it's the best way to appreciate the beauty of our country.

B Complete the sentences with the simple present or the present continuous form of the verbs in parentheses.

1. Mmm! That pizza ______________ (smell) so good!
2. Please don't talk to me now. I ______________ (do) my homework.
3. Right now, we ______________ (know) several hundred English words.
4. Miguel says he won the lottery, but I ______________ (not believe) him.
5. I ______________ (hate) hot weather because I always ______________ (feel) tired.
6. Fred ______________ (learn) how to cook. His mother ______________ (teach) him.
7. I ______________ (own) a car, but today I ______________ (take) the bus to work.
8. Carol and Aisha ______________ (belong) to the International Club.
9. Our teacher ______________ (look) angry. I wonder why.
10. This exercise ______________ (seem) really easy. I ______________ (understand) all of the sentences!

C Mark the sentence **C** for *correct* or **I** for *incorrect*. Rewrite the incorrect sentences in your notebook.

1. _____ Sorry, but I'm not understand that word.
2. _____ Right now, we look at photos from our vacation.
3. _____ Rose and Angelo are listening to a new album.
4. _____ I think that English is a very useful language.
5. _____ The onion soup is tasting too salty.
6. _____ I don't know Ali's email address.
7. _____ Mr. Jones is having a new job.
8. _____ This phone doesn't belong to me.

B UNSOLVED MYSTERIES

VOCABULARY AND GRAMMAR

A Read the article and fill in the blanks with words from the box.

can't	figure out	make sense	mysteries	solved
explanations	investigate	might	proof	theory

What Happened to Amelia Earhart?

Amelia Earhart was one of the world's greatest aviators. The story of her disappearance is one of the world's greatest **(1.)** ________________. In 1937, she wanted to show that a woman could fly a plane all the way around the world. On July 2, 1937, Earhart took off on a flight across the Pacific Ocean, and no one ever saw her again. Her plane was never found. There have been many **(2.)** ________________ for her disappearance, and some of them **(3.)** ________________, but others **(4.)** ________________ be possible. However, no one has been able to **(5.)** ________________ for sure what actually happened to her and her partner, Fred Noonan. One popular **(6.)** ________________ is that they crashed in a huge rainstorm. Many people are still very interested in the story, so they continue to **(7.)** ________________. Some believe new technology **(8.)** ________________ give us some **(9.)** ________________ about the theories. Will Earhart's disappearance finally be **(10.)** ________________?

B What do you think happened to Amelia Earhart? Read about her story online and write your answer in your notebook. Use modals.

C You are relaxing in the park with friends. Suddenly you see a strange-looking object flying in the sky. Make five statements about the object. Use each of these modals once: *may*, *might*, *could*, *can't*, *couldn't*.

1. ____
2. ____
3. ____
4. ____
5. ____

READING AND WRITING

A Read the article.

The Tungusca Mystery

It was early morning, June 30, 1908, in eastern Russia. Suddenly, a terrible explosion shook the forest in Tunguska. People fell to the ground, and all the trees for 2,000 square kilometers were knocked down. People heard the explosion 800 kilometers away, and the fire burned for many weeks.

What caused this terrible explosion? Over a century later, scientists are still trying to find the answer. Here are possible explanations:

1. A meteor: A meteor is a rock from outer space that passes into our atmosphere. Meteors can cause a lot of damage. Some of them weigh as much as 100,000 tons. If a meteor hit Earth, it would cause a huge explosion.
2. A comet: Comets are gaint balls of gas, ice, and rock with long tails. They travel through space in a regular pattern. Encke's Comet was near Earth in 1908, and it's possible that a part of it broke off and hit Earth.
3. A UFO accident: Some people believe that a spaceship, or other Unidentified Flying Object, crashed into the ground in Siberia and its engine exploded.
4. An alien attack: Another idea is that aliens (beings from another planet) attacked Earth.
5. A science experiment: Another idea is that scientists made a mistake during an experiment with electricity. A man named Nikola Tesla tried to build a "supergun" that used electricity. Maybe it was a test of his gun, and it didn't work correctly.

B Find the answers to these questions in the reading.

1. What happened? ______________________________
2. Where did it happen? ______________________________
3. When did it happen? ______________________________

C Write numbers in the boxes to match the pictures with the explanations in the reading.

D Complete the paragraph by completing the words. One of the answers will be two words.

No one has ever been able to **(1.)** f _ _ _ _ _ _ _ t what happened in Tunguska. There have been many different **(2.)** i _ _ _ _ _ _ _ _ _ _ _ _ _ n s, but there is still no clear **(3.)** e _ _ _ _ _ _ _ _ _ _ n. And how are we going to get **(4.)** p _ _ _ f? It happened over 100 years ago! Some of the explanations make **(5.)** s _ _ _ e. But some of the **(6.)** t _ _ _ _ _ _ _ s are just plain crazy. I have a feeling that this **(7.)** m _ _ _ _ _ y may never be **(8.)** s _ _ _ _ d.

E What do you think? Write your own explanation of the Tunguska mystery.

F Research and write about one of these famous mysteries: *the Loch Ness Monster*, *the Bermuda Triangle*, or *the Moai Statues of Rapa Nui*.

4

TRENDS

A HOW WE SHOP

VOCABULARY

A Match the words with the numbers.

_____ 1. 1,000 a. one point one

_____ 2. 1,000,000 b. one thousand

_____ 3. 1,000,000,000 c. one million

_____ 4. 1.1 d. one billion

B Complete the sentences with the words in the box.

~~almost~~	a lot	approximately	billion	exactly	increase	million	point	~~thousand~~	trend

1. Rio de Janeiro, Brazil is *almost* five *thousand* km from Lima, Peru.
2. There were __________ 1.4 __________ people living in China in January 2020.
3. There are __________ more Japanese restaurants here than in my hometown.
4. The graph shows an __________ in online clothing sales.
5. There was a twenty-one __________ five percent increase in delivery orders in March.
6. There are __________ 60 minutes in one hour.
7. Berlin has a population of nearly four __________.
8. My research shows a __________ toward people choosing to buy groceries online.

C Read the article and circle the correct words.

Dubai—A Shopper's Paradise

With (1.) **approximately** / **increase** three (2.) **point** / **million** people, Dubai is the largest city in the United Arab Emirates. It is also a popular place for tourists and one of the world's best places to shop.

For example, *Dubai Gold Souk* is a huge jewelry market with (3.) **about** / **more** 400 stores! Over 10 (4.) **million** / **point** people go there every year. At *Bur Dubai*—a textile market—shoppers can buy clothing and material in over a (5.) **thousand** / **nearly** different patterns and colors.

The *Burj Khalifa* is probably the most famous landmark in Dubai. It is one of the tallest skyscrapers in the world at (6.) **exactly** / **nearly** eight hundred and twenty-nine (7.) **point** / **more** eight meters. And, most importantly for shoppers, you can get there from inside the *Dubai Mall*, a huge shopping mall selling everything you can imagine. It's (8.) **nearly** / **increase** the size of 200 soccer fields!

CONVERSATION

A Match the parts.

_____ 1. I know what you're — a. I disagree.

_____ 2. I see what you — b. about that.

_____ 3. I'm not sure — c. saying, but . . .

_____ 4. That's not a bad — d. disagree.

_____ 5. I'm afraid — e. mean, but . . .

_____ 6. Sorry, — f. but I disagree.

_____ 7. I totally — g. idea, but . . .

B Unscramble the words to complete the conversation.

Melina: I'm trying to think of a good gift for my son's birthday.

Oscar: Well, what does he like? Does he have any hobbies?

Melina: Well, he keeps asking me for a video game console.

Oscar: that. / Oh, / sure / not / I'm / about

1. ____

Melina: Really, why not? It will keep him busy for hours.

Oscar: I'm / disagree. / but I / sorry, / I think / video games / lazy. / people / make

2. ____

Melina: but / I know / what / you mean, / games / good for / are / problem solving.

3. ____

Oscar: disagree. / afraid / I'm / I

4. ____

C Read the statements and give your opinion and a reason. If you disagree, use one of the expressions from **A**.

1. Young people should get an apartment after they finish high school.

   I'm afraid I disagree. Some teenagers aren't ready to live alone.

2. People shouldn't get married before they're 30 years old.

   ____

3. The best place for older people to live is with their children.

   ____

4. Playing video games makes people lazy.

   ____

5. People should live with their parents until they get married.

   ____

6. Young children should watch as much television as they want.

   ____

GRAMMAR

A Write about your friends. Use *all of*, *most of*, *a lot of*, *some of*, *a couple of*, or *none of*.

1. have a dog ______
2. like sports ______
3. like hip-hop music ______
4. are married ______
5. live near me ______
6. can drive ______

B Add the quantity expressions in parentheses to each sentence. Use *of* where necessary.

1. ______ (most) my classmates plan to go to college.
2. ______ (all) classes start at 9 a.m.
3. Only ______ (a couple) the families in this neighborhood have cars.
4. In ______ (some) countries the population is decreasing.
5. ______ (a lot) students study late at night before exams.
6. ______ (many) families have grandparents living with them.
7. I finished reading ______ (some) the books I borrowed from the library.
8. ______ (none) my friends can come to the party on Saturday.

C Write sentences about the houses using quantity expressions.

1. doors *A couple of the houses have two doors.*
2. trees ______
3. white ______
4. flowers ______
5. three windows ______
6. two floors ______

B FASHION ON DEMAND

VOCABULARY AND GRAMMAR

A Complete the sentences with the words and phrases in the box.

brands	comfortable	influencer	looks great in	suits
casual	inexpensive	look good on	style	unique

1. Margarita ______________ everything she wears.
2. That color definitely ______________ you. It's perfect.
3. I get my clothes from ______________ stores. I don't waste money on expensive ______________.
4. These pajamas feel so nice! They are very ______________.
5. Does this shirt ______________ me? Or should I buy the striped one?
6. I follow an ______________ online. I love her ______________.
7. Mario has such a ______________ look. Nobody dresses like him.
8. I wear ______________ clothes at home, but like to dress up when I go out.

B Give advice to people. Use verbs from the box.

could	had better not	ought to	should

1. I want to buy an inexpensive car.
____
2. I want to find somewhere exciting to go for a vacation.
____
3. I need to lose weight.
____
4. I have an exam tomorrow, but my friends are going to a party tonight.
____
5. I feel sick.
____

C Your friend has an important job interview tomorrow. Give them fashion advice. Use each of the expressions in **B** once.

____
____
____
____
____
____
____

READING AND WRITING

A Read the problems and the opinions below. Which opinions match which problems? Write the numbers in the correct space.

We gave readers' questions to two fashion experts. Which advice should they take?

This month: A Sense of Style

I'm a salesperson in a women's clothing store. My boss is great, but she has a very strict dress code. We have to wear long skirts, black shoes, no jewelry . . . you get the idea. It's really boring, so I'm planning to dye my hair red. What do you think?
– Lana

Opinions: _____ and _____

I love my girlfriend, but she complains a lot about my clothes. She doesn't want to go anywhere with me because I always wear old jeans and a T-shirt. I don't care about looking like some model in a fashion magazine. I just want to be comfortable! What's your advice?
– Dave

Opinions: _____ and _____

1. That's absolutely right. If she really loves you, she should listen to you and respect your feelings. If she hates your clothes, maybe she can suggest an influencer to follow who has a style you both like.
2. Sorry, but I have to side with your employer. A business wants to have a particular look, so they tell you what to wear. If you want to show off your individual style, you had better do it in your free time.
3. I'm afraid I disagree. Style is important because it shows our personality. Maybe you should find a new job.
4. I think you ought to have a serious talk with your girlfriend and explain how you feel. We all have our own unique style and taste and some of us prefer casual clothes. In my opinion, she thinks too much about appearances.

B Match the words from the article with the meanings.

_____ 1. dress code	a. agree with
_____ 2. dye	b. for one person
_____ 3. complains	c. change the color of
_____ 4. respect	d. what you must wear
_____ 5. side with	e. talks about in a bad way
_____ 6. individual	f. accepting difference without judgment

C Here's another problem like those in the article. Circle the eight spelling mistakes and write the correct spelling on the lines below.

> All my friends have more money than I do, and they spend it all on shoping for clothses. I have to save money for college, and I can't affrod to follow trennds. They never say anything about my inxpensive clothes, but I really wish I could look more uniqe. What should I do? – *Sujay*
>
> **Opinion:** You should choosse your own styel. Don't follow the crowd. Find your own look, and you'll do just fine.

1. *shopping* ________ 3. ________ 5. ________ 7. ________

2. ________ 4. ________ 6. ________ 8. ________

D Write your own opinion about one of the problems from the article. Do you agree with the experts?

5

MY NEIGHBORHOOD

A CHORES AND ERRANDS

VOCABULARY

A Put the words from the box in the correct column.

a reservation	dinner	grocery shopping	pick up	the dishes
an appointment	drop off	laundry	sweep	vacuum

do	go	make	X

B Complete the sentences with *do*, *make*, or *go* and the words from **A**. Remember: some words don't need to follow one of the verbs.

1. I usually ________________ because I'm a better cook than my roommate.
2. My brother and I ________________ every night after dinner.
3. The kitchen floor is so dirty. Could you ________________ it, please?
4. Don't forget to ________________ Emilio from soccer practice.
5. I always ________________ my wife at her office on the way to work.
6. You have a fever. Let's ________________ a doctor's ________________.
7. This carpet is covered in dust! You need to ________________!
8. She asked her assistant to ________________ at the hotel.

C Think about yourself and the people you live with now or lived with in the past. What are or were the errands and who usually does or did which?

Person	Errands
1. You	
2. ________________	
3. ________________	

CONVERSATION

A Number these sentences in order to make conversations.

1. _____ This is Fatma Aslan. I'm calling to ask about language classes at your school.
   _____ Hello. English Department. This is Alan speaking.
   _____ I can help you with that. Come to the school and we can discuss your needs.
   _____ Sure. How about 2:00?
   _____ Can I come in this afternoon?
   _____ That's perfect! Thanks.

2. _____ Could I make an appointment for next Friday, please?
   _____ Hello. Wagner College. How may I help you?
   _____ I'll be there for the 1:00 tour. Thanks!
   _____ Hi. I'd like to make an appointment to tour the college.
   _____ Of course! We have tours on Wednesdays and Fridays.
   _____ Sure. There are tours at 1:00 and 3:00 in the afternoon.

3. _____ OK. How's tomorrow at 3:00?
   _____ Professor Liang speaking.
   _____ That time isn't good for me. I have a class.
   _____ That works for me. Thank you, Professor.
   _____ Hi, Professor. This is Alma. I'm calling to reschedule our meeting.
   _____ Can you come at 5:00 today instead?

B Match the sentence halves.

_____ 1. I'm calling to	a. perfect.
_____ 2. No, that time	b. the meeting.
_____ 3. That's	c. make a hair appointment.
_____ 4. Could we	d. doesn't work for me.
_____ 5. I'd like to reschedule	e. meet at 2:00?

C Write a conversation like the one in **A**. Use your own ideas.

Other person: ______________________________

You: ______________________________

Other person: ______________________________

You: ______________________________

Other person: ______________________________

You: ______________________________

GRAMMAR

A Write a request for each situation. Use *can you*, *could you*, *will you*, *would you*, or *would you mind*.

1. You're at a job interview. You don't understand the question.

   ____

2. You're at a restaurant with your friends. You don't have enough money.

   ____

3. You're trying to study. Your brother is watching TV.

   ____

4. Your instructor is speaking very quietly. You can't hear.

   ____

5. You're cleaning your apartment with your roommate. The furniture is very heavy.

   ____

6. You're writing a paper in English. You think there are some mistakes.

   ____

7. Your friend is going grocery shopping. You need some coffee.

   ____

8. You don't have time to cook dinner for the family. Your sister said she can help but is talking on the phone.

   ____

B Agree to these requests. Choose the correct answers.

1. Would you mind going to the store for me?

   a. Yes, of course. b. No, not at all.

2. Would you drive me to my dentist appointment?

   a. I'd be glad to. b. Sorry, but I would.

3. Can you help me with my errands?

   a. Sure, no problem. b. Not at all.

4. Would you answer the phone, please?

   a. Of course. b. No, I'd be glad to.

C Circle the mistakes and rewrite the questions correctly.

1. Could you mind turning down the music?

   ____

2. Will you passing me the salt?

   ____

3. Could you closed the window, please?

   ____

4. Can you explaining that to me again?

   ____

5. Would you mind help me with this?

   ____

B GETTING AROUND

VOCABULARY AND GRAMMAR

A Unscramble the letters to make words.

1. klabalwe ______________________
2. drespasinet ______________________
3. fractif ______________________
4. lcstsiyc ______________________
5. teg radoun ______________________
6. dewlisska ______________________
7. kbei nelas ______________________
8. no tofo ______________________
9. tge ot ______________________

B Complete the sentences. Use words from **A**.

1. Drivers need to watch out for ______________ crossing the street.
2. I prefer to get around the city ______________. It's a good way to get some exercise.
3. Often, the easiest ways to ______________ a big city are by subway and by bus.
4. ______________ should always use the ______________.
5. I live in a ______________ neighborhood. I can get to all the places I need to go on foot.
6. The ______________ is horrible. I think I'll bike to work instead.
7. You can ______________ the museum by subway.
8. Don't ride your bicycle on the ______________! Those are for pedestrians only.

C Match the sentence halves.

____ 1. Our company sells chocolate	a. that runs on electricity.
____ 2. Seoul is a city	b. that teaches yoga.
____ 3. This is the movie	c. that comes from Ghana.
____ 4. It's a type of car	d. that helps you get in shape.
____ 5. A yogi is someone	e. that made me want to become an actor.
____ 6. A personal trainer is a person	f. that has a fantastic subway system.

READING AND WRITING

A Read the article.

Better Transportation for Better Neighborhoods

Two South American cities are world leaders in transportation.

In the 1970s, Curitiba was one of Brazil's fastest-growing cities, and it had serious pollution problems. The local government started several programs to reduce people's need for cars. World-famous innovations included new, extra-large buses, special new roads for buses only, and a road system that keeps highways out of the city center. This plan has been very successful. Buses come as often as every 90 seconds, so people do not have to wait very long for them. More than 1.3 million travelers take the "bus rapid transit" system in Curitiba every day.

Bogotá, Colombia, used different ideas. Many people there wanted to build a subway system, but subways are very expensive. Instead, the city built many new roads for biking and walking only. The goverment bought hundreds of buses to lighten the rush hour traffic. In 2002, the city celebrated Car-Free Day, and 7 million citizens went to work without a car. And in 2014, Car-Free Day became Car-Free Week. For a city of 7 million people, this is quite an amazing accomplishment. Every Sunday, 125 kilometers of roads are closed to cars. Every weekend, up to 2 million people in Bogotá come out to enjoy the clean air and quiet in their neighborhood.

Cities around the world can learn from these examples. Better transportation improves people's lives in many different ways.

B Now complete the chart according to the information in the article. Check (✓) the correct answers.

Which city . . .	Curitiba	Bogotá	Both	Neither
1. got a new subway system?				
2. got new buses?				
3. made roads for pedestrians and cyclists only?				
4. improved its transportation system?				
5. reduced the number of people traveling by car in the city?				
6. built special new roads for buses only?				
7. got a new airport?				
8. closes some streets once a week?				

C Unscramble the words to make sentences that give transportation facts.

1. is / the country / that / The US / a third / of / the world's / has / airports

   ______________________________.

2. subway system / the city / London / that / is / world's oldest / the / has

   ______________________________.

3. Shanghai / has / the city / is / the world's / that / train / fastest

   ______________________________.

4. subway system / Seoul / biggest / the city / has the / in the world / that / is

   ______________________________.

D Find more information about the facts in **C** online. Answer the questions.

1. How many public airports are there in the US? ______________
2. When was the London subway built? ______________
3. Shanghai's super-fast train is called the Maglev. How fast does it go? ______________
4. When did the first line open on the Seoul Subway System? ______________

E Read this email to a news website. Complete the email with the correct form of the verbs in the box.

be	become	build	buy	decrease	do (not) let	increase	make	solve

Dear Editor,

Transportation **(1.)** ______________ a serious problem in our city. Every year, people buy more cars, and the traffic **(2.)** ______________ heavier. We must do several things to **(3.)** ______________ this problem:

- **(4.)** ______________ a new train station downtown.
- **(5.)** ______________ the price of subway tickets.
- **(6.)** ______________ modern, comfortable buses.
- **(7.)** ______________ the tax on new cars.
- **(8.)** ______________ people park their cars downtown.

These ideas can **(9.)** ______________ our city a better place to live in the future.

Sincerely,
Kim Mi-Ja

F Write your own email about transportation in your town or your neighborhood.

____

____

____

____

____

____

____

____

____

____

6

GOALS

A STARTING OUT

VOCABULARY

A Write the noun form of the verbs in the table.

Verb	Noun
apply	*application*
arrange	
choose	
consider	
decide	
intend	
plan	
recommend	

B Match the sentence halves.

____ 1. Did you choose
____ 2. We need to arrange
____ 3. I intend to research
____ 4. Can you write
____ 5. I think that plan
____ 6. People always ask

a. the schools online first.
b. me what my decision is.
c. a time to talk.
d. a school yet?
e. will work very well.
f. me a letter of recommendation?

C Use the verbs and nouns from **A** to complete the sentences. Some items have more than one possible answer.

1. Did you ____________________ to any colleges yet?
2. What's your ____________________ for the future?
3. My ____________________ is to visit a few schools before I ____________________ where to go.
4. Let's ____________________ a time to talk about your ____________________ letter.
5. Which school is your first ____________________?
6. Do you ____________________ to take a year off before college?
7. I don't know which classes to ____________________! They all sound so interesting.
8. Do you ____________________ going to a college close to home or moving far away?

CONVERSATION

A Match the sentence halves.

____ 1. How	a. hear that.
____ 2. That's	b. call me.
____ 3. You must be	c. disappointing.
____ 4. I'm sorry to	d. disappointed.
____ 5. If you want to talk,	e. too bad.

B Number the sentences in order to make conversations.

1. ____ I am. But at least I got into two other schools.
   ____ Hi, Tarik. What's happening with your college applications?
   ____ I didn't get into my first-choice school.
   ____ That's too bad. You must be disappointed.
   ____ Well, that's good!

2. ____ Seven. And they're all good schools.
   ____ I'm feeling stressed about getting all of my applications done.
   ____ Well, if you want to talk, just let me know. Maybe I can help.
   ____ Hey, Ava! How are you?
   ____ How many schools are you applying to?

3. ____ Not great. I just lost my job.
   ____ If there's anything I can do, let me know.
   ____ Oh, no! I'm so sorry to hear that.
   ____ How's it going, Kazuo?
   ____ Thanks.

C Write a conversation in which people respond to bad news and offer to help. Use your own ideas and the expressions in **A**.

A: ______________________________

B: ______________________________

A: ______________________________

B: ______________________________

A: ______________________________

GRAMMAR

A Match the halves.

_____ 1. I just heard the doorbell ring.	a. meet in front of the library at 2:00.
_____ 2. It's OK if you forgot your wallet.	b. sandwich and a green tea, please.
_____ 3. We're going to	c. Oslo this summer.
_____ 4. I'm going to go to	d. I'll answer the door.
_____ 5. Luis is going to use his	e. scholarship to study English.
_____ 6. I'll have a chicken	f. I'll lend you some money.

B Complete the sentences with *will* or the correct form of *be going to*.

1. I'm really hungry . . . I know! I ____________________ order some Chinese food.
2. I already planned the menu. We ____________________ have Mexican food tonight.
3. She ____________________ visit Elia in Sydney in March.
4. That box looks heavy! I ____________________ help you carry it.
5. On Friday, I ____________________ have dinner with Fabiana at an Italian restaurant.
6. Do you need someone to fix it? I ____________________ do it for you.
7. I'm ____________________ the movie theater at 8:00.
8. Does she drink coffee? I ____________________ get her one, too.

C Your friend is making the following statements. Write a response to each one.

1. The phone's ringing.
   I'll get it!
2. I'm hungry.
   ____
3. I need a ride to the airport.
   ____
4. I'm thirsty.
   ____
5. I'm running late.
   ____
6. My laptop is broken.
   ____

B AFTER GRADUATION

VOCABULARY AND GRAMMAR

A Unscramble the words to make sentences.

1. a / get into / she'll / college / good / probably

______________________________.

2. before / maybe / work for / I'll / college / a year

______________________________.

3. internship / for / he'll / apply / probably / an

______________________________.

4. she / definitely / going to / join / the team / isn't

______________________________.

5. maybe / my teacher / write / will / a letter of recommendation

______________________________.

6. move to / they'll / definitely / Osaka / when / college / she finishes

______________________________.

B Complete the paragraph with words and expressions from the box.

be my own boss	did an internship	in the near future	take time off
create a resume	go back to school	someday	opportunity

Now that I am graduating from college, I have to start thinking about my future. **(1.)** ______________, I'd like to get a job. This is my top priority at the moment. Before I can do that, I need to **(2.)** ______________ to send to the businesses I'm interested in working for. Last year, I **(3.)** ______________ with a chef at a local restaurant and I really liked it. This year, I'm looking for a full-time job at a restaurant downtown.

At some point, I think I will want to **(4.)** ______________ and travel around the world. Chefs work a lot, and I will need a break. In addition, I would like the **(5.)** ______________ to visit other countries to learn about their traditional food. I've heard Ethiopian food is great!

Eventually, I would like to own a restaurant and **(6.)** ______________. To do that, I want to **(7.)** ______________ and get a business degree. There's more to being a restaurant owner than just being able to cook. I have a lot to learn, but I think I will be able to do it all **(8.)** ______________!

C Make predictions about the person in **B**. What do you think she will do? Use *definitely* and *probably* in your answers.

1. ______________________________
2. ______________________________
3. ______________________________
4. ______________________________

READING AND WRITING

A Read the article from a student news website.

New Graduates Talk About the Future

After the City College graduation ceremony yesterday, we talked to three students about their plans and their dreams.

Jameela Brown: "I worked so hard for four years. I need a break now! I majored in biology and chemistry, and I had a summer job in a day care center. I'm going to take a year off before I start medical school. My plan is to travel and do volunteer work in West Africa. I'll be a doctor someday, but I'm not sure what kind of doctor I'll be."

Jennie Min: "I studied business, and it was easy for me to find a job. Next month I'll move to New York to start work at a large corporation. But I don't really want to spend my whole life working for a company. I hope I can start my own business—maybe something with food. I love cooking! In college, I cooked dinner for my roommates every night."

Shane Peterson: "Wow! Four years really went fast. I can't believe it's graduation day! My major was computer science, but I spent all my free time playing music. I played guitar in two different bands. I also play electronic music, using computers. I have job interviews with three software companies next week. I'm not worried about getting a job, but I really want to play music, too. That's my biggest dream."

B Match the words from the article with the meanings.

_____ 1. day care center
_____ 2. volunteer
_____ 3. corporation
_____ 4. major
_____ 5. band
_____ 6. software

a. business
b. music group
c. work for free
d. main subject you choose to study in college
e. computer programs
f. a place that takes care of children while their parents work

C Complete this chart with information from the article.

Name	Major	College Job / Hobby	Dream	Plans
Jameela	*biology and chemistry*			
Jennie				*- move to New York* *- work for a large corporation*
Shane				

D Complete the sentences with the correct form of the verbs in the box.

become	get	have	learn	start	work

I think Jameela **(1.)** ________________ very interesting experiences in West Africa. She will be prepared because she **(2.)** ________________ in a day care center. She **(3.)** ________________ a lot from that job. I think she **(4.)** ________________ a doctor for children. I predict she **(5.)** ________________ a job in a foreign country, or maybe she **(6.)** ________________ an organization to help sick children.

E Write your predictions for Jennie and Shane.

Jennie:

____

____

____

____

____

____

Shane:

____

____

____

____

____

____

F Write predictions for your own future.

____

____

____

____

____

____

7

CELEBRATIONS

A PARTIES

VOCABULARY

A Unscramble the letters to write party words.

1. tinive ______________
2. braleceet ______________
3. shot ______________
4. anlp ______________
5. stuegs ______________
6. goraniez ______________
7. ttndea ______________
8. cordetea ______________
9. wroth a trypa ______________
10. teg geettroh ______________

B Use the words in the box to complete the sentences.

attend	get	hosted	planned
decorated	guests	invited	throws

Last week, I **(1.)** ______________ a surprise birthday party at my apartment for my sister, Inez. I **(2.)** ______________ her friends to **(3.)** ______________ together at our place. Everyone that I invited responded and said they could **(4.)** ______________. On the big day, Inez's boyfriend took her out to dinner, and I **(5.)** ______________ our apartment with flowers and colorful balloons. The **(6.)** ______________ arrived, and then Inez walked into the room. Everyone shouted, "Surprise!" Inez was shocked. She could not believe that I **(7.)** ______________ the whole thing without her knowing! Everyone had a great time. I hope she **(8.)** ______________ a party for my birthday next month, but not a surprise party. I hate surprises.

C Write a plan for a party you want to host.

1. What are you celebrating?

____

2. When are you getting together?

____

3. How many guests are you inviting?

____

4. How will you decorate the room?

____

CONVERSATION

A Unscramble the words to make invitations and responses. Remember to use correct punctuation.

1. **A:** want / me / with / to / do / you / go

   ____?

   B: I'd / to / love / sure

   ____.

2. **A:** how'd / like / you / to / go / me / with

   ____?

   B: sorry / I'm / I can't / but / plans / have / I

   ____.

3. **A:** want / you / do / study / together / to

   ____?

   B: I can't / work / unfortunately / have to / I

   ____.

4. **A:** on Wednesday / how'd / like / you / see / to / a movie

   ____?

   B: love / I'd / busy / to / I'm / but / that day

   ____.

B Number the sentences (1–6) in order to make conversations.

Conversation 1:

____ Great! When is it?

____ Do you want to go with me?

____ That sounds like fun.

____ Did you hear? James and Suki are having a party.

____ On Saturday. It's a costume party.

____ I'd love to, but I'm busy that day.

Conversation 2:

____ He's a great actor. I'll check it out.

____ I'm going to see it on Friday night with my brother. Would you like to go with us?

____ That sounds great. I'd love to come.

____ Oh, really? What is it?

____ *Spider-Man: Far From Home* with Jon Favreau.

____ There's a new movie playing at the Park Cinema.

C Look at the schedules and write conversations in your notebook. Use the information below.

Liza's schedule:

Friday
Bill's barbecue 7:30
Saturday
clean the house grocery shopping

Danielle's schedule:

Friday
work 2–10 PM
Saturday
tennis with Lauren and Roberto 12:00

1. Liza invites Danielle to a barbecue. Danielle can't go.
2. Danielle invites Liza to play tennis. Liza accepts.

GRAMMAR

A Match the statements and responses in each group.

1.

_____ **1.** I don't have a soccer ball.	**a.** So am I.
_____ **2.** I'm not on the soccer team.	**b.** Me neither.
_____ **3.** I like to watch soccer on TV.	**c.** I do, too.
_____ **4.** I'm a good tennis player.	**d.** Neither am I.

2.

_____ **1.** I don't like to celebrate my birthday.	**a.** I'm not either.
_____ **2.** I'm not comfortable in big groups.	**b.** Me, too.
_____ **3.** I like to go to the gym.	**c.** I am, too.
_____ **4.** I'm a good dancer.	**d.** Neither do I.

3.

_____ **1.** I'm going to the library now.	**a.** So do I.
_____ **2.** I'm not going to study tomorrow.	**b.** I don't either.
_____ **3.** I don't like studying on weekends.	**c.** Me neither.
_____ **4.** I like sleeping late on weekends.	**d.** Me, too.

B Complete the responses with *either*, *neither*, *so*, or *too*.

1. I'm not going to the party on Friday.	I'm not _____________.
2. Sarah is going to the dance at school.	_____________ am I.
3. She's going to get there early.	Me, _____________.
4. She's not going to walk home.	Me _____________.
5. Anthony is a great musician.	_____________ am I.
6. I love reading.	I do, _____________.
7. I have two younger sisters.	_____________ do I.
8. We don't have a pet.	We don't _____________.

C Write short responses agreeing with these statements.

1. I like rock music. ______________________________

2. I never stay up after midnight. ______________________________

3. I often have tea with breakfast. ______________________________

4. I don't have a dog. ______________________________

5. I eat a lot of vegetables. ______________________________

6. I don't like to wake up early. ______________________________

7. I want to learn to speak Portuguese. ______________________________

8. I'm going to a restaurant tonight. ______________________________

B FESTIVALS AND HOLIDAYS

VOCABULARY AND GRAMMAR

A Complete the chart.

Verb	Noun	Noun (person)
compete		
	participation	
		performer

B Circle the correct answers.

1. The Harbin Ice Festival **takes place** / **participates** every winter in northern China.
2. A lot of actors **perform** / **performances** at the Sibiu International Theatre Festival in Romania.
3. My mother is going to be a **race** / **competitor** in the Tokyo Marathon next year.
4. Are you going to **participate** / **participant** in the games?
5. Can you win **prizes** / **competition** or is the quiz just for fun?
6. The Aste Nagusia festival in Bilbao celebrates the **traditions** / **participation** of the local people.
7. Mexican families **gather** / **participate** to remember family members on the Day of the Dead.
8. In New York City, there are musical **competes** / **performances** in Times Square on New Year's Eve.

C Match the sentence halves.

_____ 1. Please wash your hands after — a. you come home tonight, please.
_____ 2. Tell your brother to buy milk before — b. after I have dinner.
_____ 3. I always brush my teeth — c. we went for a cup of coffee.
_____ 4. Before the game starts, — d. you ride your bike.
_____ 5. Wear a helmet when — e. the players jog around the field.
_____ 6. Be quiet when — f. he gets home from work.
_____ 7. After the movie finished, — g. we'll exchange gifts.
_____ 8. After my cousins arrive, — h. you use the bathroom.

D Complete the text with *before*, *after*, or *when*.

You need to prepare for weeks **(1.)** ____________________ you sing in public. **(2.)** ____________________ I walk out on the stage, I always smile at the audience. **(3.)** ____________________ that, I take a minute to relax **(4.)** ____________________ I start singing. **(5.)** ____________________ I begin singing, I need to be completely calm. I enjoy talking to the audience outside of the theater **(6.)** ____________________ the show is over.

READING AND WRITING

A Read the article.

CELEBRATE MARDI GRAS IN NEW ORLEANS!

Mardi Gras, which means *Fat Tuesday*, takes place on a Tuesday in February or March. When Mardi Gras begins, people gather in the streets to watch over 70 parades of beautiful and interesting floats and musical performances. Come join us in New Orleans for a festival you'll never forget!

Tips for visitors:

Plan ahead. Many hotels start taking reservations for Mardi Gras in August. To get the room you want, call early. Don't wait until January!

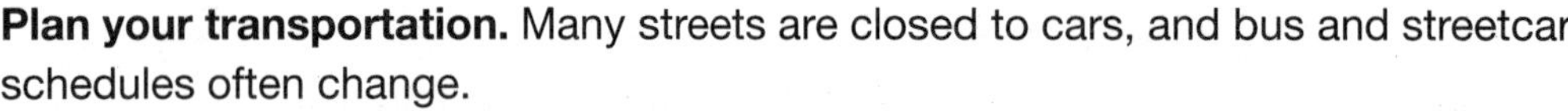

Plan your transportation. Many streets are closed to cars, and bus and streetcar schedules often change.

Get there early. Plan to arrive about four hours before any big parade. For the popular Sunday night parade, find a space in the morning. Plan your clothing carefully. You might need a jacket, sunglasses, an umbrella, or all three.

Participate and celebrate. Catch Mardi Gras "throws," or the things that people throw from the floats. Jump up to catch beads, coins, cups, and toy animals. Bring a bag to hold all of the treasures you collect.

For more information, contact the New Orleans Visitors' Bureau.

B Circle **T** for *true* or **F** for *false*. Then write the information from the article that helped you find the answer.

1. The weather is always good in New Orleans at this time of the year. **T** **F**

____

2. Some of the parades are very crowded. **T** **F**

____

3. You should make your hotel reservations for Mardi Gras in February. **T** **F**

____

4. You can get free beads and toys. **T** **F**

____

5. The parades all happen on the same day. **T** **F**

____

6. Transportation to the parades is sometimes a problem. **T** **F**

____

C Complete the paragraph with vocabulary from Lesson B. There may be more than one possible answer.

The Edinburgh Fringe is the biggest arts festival in the world. People travel to the Scottish capital from all over the world to see drama, comedy, or music **(1.)** ____________________. A lot of actors, comedians, and musicians from different countries **(2.)** ____________________ at the festival. Comedians have a chance of winning the famous Edinburgh Comedy Awards **(3.)** ____________________. There are three different **(4.)** ____________________; the biggest, for best comedy show, is £10,000. **(5.)** ____________________ work very hard, often doing three or four shows every day for 25 days!

D Read the information and fill in the spaces with *before* or *after*.

Carnival is a very colorful and interesting festival in Venice, but it gets very crowded. **(1.)** ____________________ you arrive, you should reserve a hotel room. Then, **(2.)** ____________________ you arrive, get the most up-to-date schedule for the festival. Sometimes it changes. The most important events are the masquerade balls, or costume parties. Do your research, and buy tickets to the events several months **(3.)** ____________________ Carnival begins. **(4.)** ____________________ you get tickets, you have to find a costume and mask. People sometimes bring their costumes with them, but others wait until **(5.)** ____________________ they arrive to buy one. During Carnival, many people continue to dance in the streets **(6.)** ____________________ the parties end.

E Think about a festival in your city or country. Write advice for visitors.

____

____

____

____

____

____

____

____

____

____

8

ONCE UPON A TIME

A WHAT'S THE STORY ABOUT?

VOCABULARY

A Complete the sentences with the words in the box.

based on	character	easy to follow	predictable
best-selling	director	fiction	takes place

1. My favorite ____________ in the book is the kind grandmother.
2. Did you know that movie we watched last week was ____________ a book?
3. The novel *Winter in Madrid* ____________ in Spain in the 1940s.
4. She is my favorite ____________. Her movies are so interesting.
5. Don't worry. The story is very ____________. I understood everything.
6. It was so ____________. I guessed the ending right away.
7. She doesn't like to read ____________. She prefers books about science and politics.
8. My cousin is a successful author. He writes ____________ crime novels.

B Match the sentences and sentence halves.

____ 1. This show is so unpredictable!
____ 2. I love the main character.
____ 3. What a boring show that was!
____ 4. The special effects were
____ 5. That movie is based
____ 6. Shakespeare's play *Romeo and Juliet* tells
____ 7. That movie was hard to follow.

a. She's so funny.
b. the story of a young couple in love.
c. on a short story.
d. very realistic. The aliens seemed real!
e. It was so predictable.
f. I didn't understand the ending.
g. You never know what will happen next.

C Answer the questions about yourself. Write complete sentences.

1. What TV show, movie, or book <u>don't</u> you like? Why? ____________

____

2. Who is your favorite character in a book you have read? ____________

____

3. Do you like fiction books? Why or why not? ____________

____

CONVERSATION

A Unscramble the words to make statements and questions. Remember to use the correct punctuation.

1. Wow! / serious / you / are
   Wow! Are you serious?
2. happened / what / next
   ____
3. heard / just / I / amazing / an / story
   ____
4. about / it / what's
   ____
5. did / do / he / next / what
   ____
6. take / where / place / it / does
   ____
7. about / story / it's / a / driver / race car / a
   ____

B Number the sentences to make a conversation.

1 I just read an unbelievable story.
2 What's it about?
____ Yes, really. They must have been so scared.
____ What happens after that?
____ It's a story about a group of hikers.
____ No, it's a true story.
____ Well, they get stuck in a snowstorm.
____ Oh, I love true stories. What happens?
____ Well, in the end . . .
____ Is it fiction?
____ Oh, no! Really? That sounds scary.

C Answer the questions about one of your favorite stories.

1. Where does the story take place?
   ____
2. What happens at the beginning of the story?
   ____
3. What happens after some time passes?
   ____
4. What surprising things do you learn about the characters?
   ____
5. How does the story end?
   ____

GRAMMAR

A Write what you were doing at these times.

1. yesterday / 3:00 pm *I was sitting in my office.*
2. last night / 10:00 pm ____________________
3. this morning / 7:00 am ____________________
4. last Friday / 3:00 pm ____________________
5. last Saturday / 2:00 pm ____________________
6. yesterday / 5:00 pm ____________________

B Match the questions and answers.

_____ 1. What were you doing at 8:00 this morning?
_____ 2. Was she studying in the library earlier?
_____ 3. What was she studying?
_____ 4. Were you both at the beach last summer?
_____ 5. Were they listening to music?

a. Yes, she was.
b. I was taking the subway to work.
c. She was studying math.
d. Yes, we were.
e. Yes, they were.

C Last night the Macedo family got an exciting phone call. They won $1,000,000 in the lottery! What were they doing when they got the call? Look at the picture and complete the sentences.

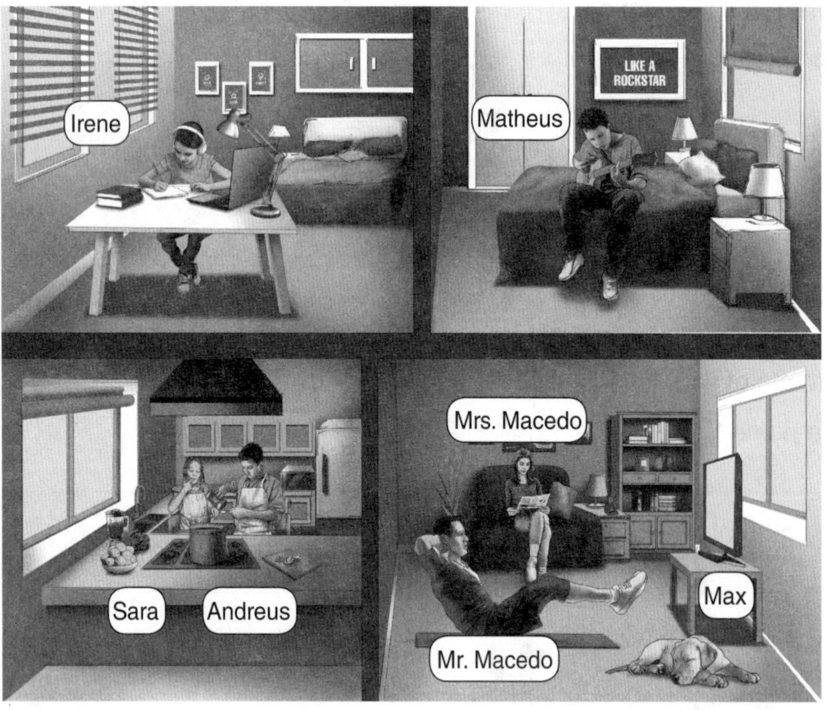

1. Irene ____________________
2. Matheus ____________________
3. Andreus ____________________
4. Sara ____________________
5. Mrs. Macedo ____________________
6. Mr. Macedo ____________________
7. Max ____________________

B MODERN FAIRY TALES

VOCABULARY AND GRAMMAR

A Complete the words.

1. a n ___ ___ e ___ t
2. t ___ a ___ i t ___ ___ ___ a l
3. m ___ g ___ c
4. e ___ ___ l
5. c l ___ ___ e r
6. b ___ a v ___
7. s u c ___ e ___ d
8. i ___ c ___ e ___ i ___ l e
9. d ___ s ___ o ___ ___ r s

B Complete the book description with words from **A**.

Stardust is one of my favorite fiction books. It tells the story of a young man named Tristan living in a small village in **(1.)** ________________ times. Tristan promises to find a fallen star for the girl he loves. But, when he goes to look for it, he **(2.)** ________________ that the star is **(3.)** ________________ and has turned into a beautiful girl. He tries to take her home to the one he loves, but there are some **(4.)** ________________ characters who also want the star-girl. What I really enjoyed about the book is that it seems like a simple fairy tale, but the more you read, the more you realize the plot is actually very **(5.)** ________________. For example, the author includes some interesting creatures from **(6.)** ________________ Scottish folktales from hundreds of years ago. He probably did a lot of research before writing the story.

C Complete the sentences with the adverb form of the words in the box.

deep	fluent	shy
different	good	strange
~~eloquent~~	instant	usual

1. She speaks so ___*eloquently*___ about her passion for writing.
2. It hurt me ________________ when you shouted at me last night.
3. We need to do this ________________ than the others if we want to be noticed.
4. When I heard that laugh, I ________________ knew it was you!
5. Samuel lives in Seoul and speaks Korean ________________ now.
6. The boy acted ________________ at the party. He doesn't like speaking to strangers.
7. I ________________ bring an umbrella in my bag, but I forgot it today.
8. I think you will do very ________________ in the competition.
9. Is Julia OK? She was acting ________________ in our meeting.

READING AND WRITING

A Read the story. Number the parts (1–7) in the correct order.

Juha Stories

In many parts of the Middle East and North Africa, people love to tell old stories about a man named Juha. Is he clever or not? Read one of the Juha stories and decide.

_____ Finally, Juha came home. He entered the house and told his wife, "I'm very hungry! Where is the expensive meat that I bought for my dinner?"

_____ "Oh, Juha," she said, "I'm so sorry. The cat ate the meat!"

_____ Juha asked his wife, "If this is the cat, where's the meat? And if this is the meat, where's the cat?"

_____ One day, Juha bought three pounds of expensive meat at the market. He brought it home and said to his wife, "Please cook this meat for my dinner." Then he went out to see his friends.

_____ Juha's wife roasted the meat and waited a long time for her husband. But, he didn't come back, and she got very hungry. "Well," she thought, "I'll just take a little piece." She cut off a small piece of meat and ate it.

_____ Juha got angry. He picked up the cat and weighed it on his scale. The cat weighed precisely three pounds.

_____ But Juha still didn't come back. His wife ate another little piece of the meat, and then another, and another. Soon, there wasn't any meat.

B Write the words from the story next to the correct meaning.

1. in the end _______________
2. went into _______________
3. spent money on _______________
4. a measurement of weight _______________
5. cooked in an oven _______________
6. measured how heavy something is _______________
7. a machine for measuring how heavy something is _______________
8. exactly _______________

C Read the story again. Then answer the questions.

1. What kind of person is Juha?

____

____

2. What kind of person is Juha's wife?

____

____

3. In your opinion, what is the lesson of this story?

____

____

4. Is Juha clever or not? Explain your answer.

____

____

D Read the story and fill in the correct verb forms. Use the simple past or past continuous.

The Tortoise and the Eagle

One day, a tortoise **(1.** sleep**)** ______________ in the sun. He **(2.** open**)** ______________ his eyes and **(3.** see**)** ______________ an eagle. The eagle **(4.** fly**)** ______________ high in the sky. "I want to fly like that!" the tortoise **(5.** say**)** ______________. The eagle **(6.** hear**)** ______________ him and **(7.** agree**)** ______________ to help him. The eagle **(8.** pick up**)** ______________ the tortoise, and they **(9.** go**)** ______________ up. When they **(10.** fly**)** ______________ very high in the sky, the eagle **(11.** say**)** ______________, "Now, try it yourself." He **(12.** open**)** ______________ his claws, and the poor tortoise **(13.** fall**)** ______________ to the ground.

The lesson: *Wishes can be dangerous!*

E Write a fairy tale or popular story from your country. Does it have a lesson? If so, what is it?

____

____

____

____

____

____

____

____

____

____

____

9

WORK

A SKILLS AND QUALITIES

VOCABULARY

A Solve this crossword puzzle.

Across

1. friendly and nice
2. full of useful information
4. brave; unafraid
5. able to change directions easily
6. working (well) alone

Down

1. always on time
3. able to get things done quickly and correctly
4. careful

B Complete the sentences with words from **A**.

1. You need to speak to customers a lot, so you must be friendly and ______________.
2. He works well in groups but also ______________.
3. She's very ______________; she works quickly and doesn't make mistakes.
4. You must be ______________ because class starts at exactly 8:00 am.
5. You have to be very ______________ because the job can be dangerous.

CONVERSATION

A Match the questions and answers.

____ 1. Can you work independently?
____ 2. Are you adventurous?
____ 3. Do you have any experience writing a blog?
____ 4. Do you have any questions?
____ 5. Where did you go to school?
____ 6. When can you start?

a. Right away!
b. Yes. Does the job involve travel?
c. Yes. I love trying new things.
d. Yes, I can. For example, I worked from home in my last job.
e. I was a student at the University of Lima.
f. Yes. I write one for my college's website.

B Unscramble the words to make sentences.

1. soon / touch / I'll / in / be

____.

2. great / be / here / it's / to

____.

3. my / it's / pleasure

____.

4. majoring / English / in / I'm

____.

5. hearing / you / I / forward / to / look / from

____.

C Look at the job ad. Imagine you are at an interview for this job. Write the interviewer's questions and your answers. Use the questions in **A** to help you.

Interviewer: ____
____

You: ____
____

Interviewer: ____
____

You: ____
____

Interviewer: ____
____

You: ____

Interviewer: ____

You: ____

WE NEED
A TOUR GUIDE!

Requirements:

- Personable
- Foreign language skills
- Experience leading tours
- Knowledgeable about local area

Call Excel Travel: 555-4231

GRAMMAR

A Write the past participle of each verb. Use your dictionary if necessary.

1. go __________
2. be __________
3. have __________
4. study __________
5. drink __________
6. sleep __________
7. come __________
8. read __________
9. take __________
10. think __________
11. know __________
12. do __________

B Look at the lists and write sentences about what the people have done so far and what they haven't done yet.

Ina's list:

1. call Ms. Ramirez *She hasn't called Ms. Ramirez.*
2. go to the bank ✓ __________
3. write email to Marco __________
4. read the report __________
5. prepare for meeting ✓ __________

Mr. and Mrs. Silva's list:

1. take the kids to school ✓ *They have taken the kids to school.*
2. go shopping __________
3. clean the house ✓ __________
4. make lunch __________
5. wash the dishes __________

Juan's list:

1. do homework ✓ __________
2. buy a dictionary ✓ __________
3. study for the test __________
4. get new textbook __________
5. have dinner with Anne __________

C Write sentences about how long you have participated in these activities. Use *for* or *since*.

1. be married *I've been married for three years.*
2. study English __________
3. know my best friend __________
4. have this shirt __________
5. be at this school __________
6. be in this class __________
7. live in this city __________
8. have this hairstyle __________
9. live in my house __________

B DREAM JOBS

VOCABULARY AND GRAMMAR

A Match the words and their meanings.

_____ 1. well paid	a. very tiring
_____ 2. exhausting	b. dangerous
_____ 3. glamorous	c. making a lot of money
_____ 4. hazardous	d. requiring a lot of time or energy
_____ 5. demanding	e. bringing good feelings because of effort
_____ 6. rewarding	f. exciting and attractive

B Complete the sentences. Write the simple past or present perfect form of the verbs.

1. **A:** (like) ____________ you ____________ the second book in the series?
   B: I (not read) ____________ it yet.
2. **A:** How long (know) ____________ you ____________ Alice?
   B: Alice and I (know) ____________ each other since elementary school.
3. **A:** I (see) ____________ a new movie yesterday.
   B: (enjoy) ____________ you ____________ it?
4. **A:** What (study) ____________ you ____________ last year?
   B: I (study) ____________ biology.
5. **A:** (be) ____________ you ever ____________ to Brazil?
   B: Yes. I (go) ____________ there to study Portuguese last year.
6. **A:** (finish) ____________ you ____________ your math homework yet?
   B: Yes. I (finish) ____________ it this morning.

C Choose the correct answer to complete the sentences.

1. I **ate / have eaten** at this restaurant hundreds of times.
2. My mother **walked / has walked** around the park on Tuesday.
3. I **thought / have thought** you knew where you were going.
4. They **traveled / have traveled** to Athens more than ten times now!
5. We **did / have done** yoga for the first time last month.
6. Selina **moved / has moved** to Moscow in 2018.
7. Paco **never had / has never had** Thai food before.
8. Gina **worked / has worked** at Toy Co. since she was 23.

READING AND WRITING

A Read the article.

You've never met Ryan Hayes, and you don't know his name, but you know his voice. He records movie trailers. When you hear *Coming soon to a theater near you . . .*, that's Ryan!

"Yes, it's true," he says. "I'm the voice talent for West Coast Audio." Millions of people hear his voice every year. "I try to make the movie sound as exciting and interesting as possible. I want to grab the viewer's attention from the first word."

Ryan has a flexible schedule, but he has to practice a lot. Sometimes he has to record the same script over and over. "My voice has to sound the same at the end of eight hours." So Ryan is very cautious with his voice. "I don't go outside in cold weather, and I drink a lot of hot water with honey. I never go on roller coasters because I might scream and hurt my voice!"

How did Ryan get his job? "A friend told me about it. I watched a lot of movie trailers, and then I made a recording of my voice. After I emailed it to West Coast Audio, I called them every week for a month!"

He's been doing this job for five years now, and he loves it. "It's fun and rewarding! And sometimes I even get to meet movie stars." Plus, people are always surprised when they hear about Ryan's job. They say, "Really? That's your voice? I thought it sounded familiar!"

B Complete the chart with information from the reading.

Name:	
Job:	
Company:	
Good parts of his job:	
Bad parts of his job:	

C Write what these words in the reading refer to.

1. *his* in line 5 refers to ______________________
2. *it* in line 16 refers to ______________________
3. *it* in line 17 refers to ______________________
4. *it* in line 21 refers to ______________________

D Complete the paragraph with the words in the box and the simple past or present perfect form of the verbs in parentheses.

demanding	glamorous	rewarding
exhausting	hazardous	well paid

When Dan **(1. be)** ________________ 33, he was tired of his job. He **(2. work)** ________________ as a lawyer in downtown Chicago, and though his job was **(3.)** ________________ and his lifestyle was **(4.)** ________________, he didn't think the money was worth the stress. He was ready to leave. After he quit, he **(5. travel)** ________________ around Eastern Europe for a month. While he was in Bulgaria, he **(6. meet)** ________________ a carpenter who **(7. own)** ________________ his own business. The man spoke about the freedom he had and how he loved working outdoors. This conversation made Dan think, and when he got home, he **(8. decide)** ________________ to start his own roofing business. Now, he **(9. be)** ________________ his own boss for the past three years. Dan and his crew replace and repair roofs on people's homes. "The job can be physically **(10.)** ________________," says Dan. Standing on a roof, carrying heavy tools for many hours is **(11.)** ________________, but Dan says he **(12. become)** ________________ stronger over time. The work is also **(13.)** ________________ sometimes. Dan told us that he **(14. have)** ________________ almost ________________ a couple of accidents on the job. "You need to be very cautious, but seeing a finished project at the end of the week is so **(15.)** ________________," he says. "I **(16. be)** ________________ never ________________ happier at any other job. You will never see me in an office again. That's for sure."

E Write a job ad. Use vocabulary from the unit.

____

____

____

____

____

____

____

____

____

____

____

10

STAY IN TOUCH

A ON A CALL

VOCABULARY

A Complete the phrases.

1. s ___ e ___ d t ___ ___ e
2. g ___ ___ i ___ t ___ ___ c h
3. c ___ e c ___ y ___ u r p h ___ n ___
4. c h ___ ___ k y o ___ r e ___ a ___ l
5. r ___ t ___ r ___ a c ___ l ___
6. g ___ t a t ___ x ___
7. o ___ s ___ l ___ ___ t
8. I ___ ___ n't h ___ v e a s ___ g n ___ l

B Match the words to complete the expressions.

____ 1. pass	a. call
____ 2. stay in	b. a signal.
____ 3. check your	c. meeting
____ 4. make a	d. messages
____ 5. attend a	e. on mute.
____ 6. My phone is	f. time
____ 7. get a	g. touch
____ 8. I can't get	h. text

C Complete the sentences with phrases from **A**.

1. I always put my phone ____________________ when I am in a meeting.
2. I often ____________________ on my phone when I'm bored.
3. ____________________ with me tomorrow, and I'll give you more information about the job.
4. Did you ____________________? I sent the documents to you this morning.
5. I'm sorry, but I need to ____________________ that I missed. I'll be right back.
6. Please don't ____________________ during class. It's rude.
7. Is your phone working? ____________________ here.
8. Did you ____________________ from Valeria about her party on Saturday?

CONVERSATION

A Unscramble the statements and questions. Remember to use the correct punctuation.

1. Karla / there / is / hi

   ____?

2. may / Sunni / speak / hello / to / I

   ____?

3. Mark / is / hello / this

   ____.

4. ask / calling / I / who's / may

   ____?

5. like / message / to / would / leave / you / a

   ____?

6. moment / hang on / you / can / a / for

   ____?

7. hold / you / second / could / a / for

   ____?

B Number the sentences in order to make conversations.

Conversation 1: A teacher is calling a student back.

_____ Will we be able to use our dictionaries during the test?
_____ Right. What did you want to talk to me about?
__1__ Hannah, this is Professor Gayle.
_____ Oh? What is it?
_____ Certainly. I always let students use dictionaries.
_____ Oh, hi, Professor Gayle. I left you a message earlier.
_____ I have a question about tomorrow's exam.
_____ OK. Thanks. That's good to know.
_____ See you tomorrow, Hannah. Please get in touch by email if you need anything else.

Conversation 2: Three friends are talking on the phone.

_____ Sure. No problem.
__1__ Hi, Rob. How are you?
_____ Hi Aida. Can I call you back later? Someone is on the other line, and I need to speak to him.
__2__ Hey, Kenan. I'm fine, thanks. Are you ready for tomorrow's test?
_____ Hello?
_____ Yeah, I studied already. (Phone beeps) Rob, could you hold for a second?
_____ Hi, Kenan. This is Aida.

C In your notebook, write your own phone conversation.

GRAMMAR

A Unscramble the statements and questions. Remember to use the correct punctuation.

1. I / later / called back / would / be / it / OK / if
____
2. problem / no / sure
____
3. would / if / mind / you / seat / to / another / moved / I
____
4. vegan / meal / have / we / may / the
____
5. but / use / need / I / sorry / to / now / it
____
6. no / all / at / not
____
7. go / certainly / ahead
____
8. mind / do / you / I / if / borrow / pencil / a
____

B Complete the conversations.

1. **A:** Would it ______________ I called back this evening?
B: ______________, no ______________.
2. **A:** Do you ______________ I sit here?
B: No, not ______________. Go ______________.
3. **A:** Would you ______________ I turned a fan on?
B: ______________, go ______________.
4. **A:** ______________ take this seat?
B: ______________, but that's my friend's seat.

C Read each situation. Use the verbs in parentheses to ask permission.

1. You are on an airplane. You want to have the vegetarian meal. Ask the flight attendant for one. (have)
____
2. You are waiting for an important call, but phones aren't allowed in class. Ask permission. (check)
____
3. You are in a meeting listening to a presentation. You have a question. Ask the presenter. (ask)
____
4. You are at a cafe. You want to know if they have any caffeine-free drinks. (tell, have)
____

B ALWAYS CONNECTED

VOCABULARY AND GRAMMAR

A Match the words and meanings.

____ 1. addicted to	a. give permission to happen
____ 2. allow	b. make available to be read or seen (online)
____ 3. ban	c. reply
____ 4. delete	d. decrease (the volume, temperature, etc.)
____ 5. ignore	e. not listen to, read, or notice anymore
____ 6. post	f. can't stop using or doing something
____ 7. be distracted by	g. impolite
____ 8. rude	h. remove (permanently)
____ 9. turn down	i. increase (the volume, temperature, etc.)
____ 10. turn up	j. stop letting (something) happen
____ 11. pay attention to	k. focus on
____ 12. respond	l. unable to think or focus because of something

B Complete the sentences with vocabulary from **A**.

1. Some people want to ________________ cell phone use in restaurants.
2. When someone is talking loudly on their cell phone, I try to ________________ them.
3. Some people are ________________ phone games. They play them for hours each day!
4. Sometimes we spend so much time looking down at our phone screens that we don't ________________ what's going on around us.
5. People sometimes ________________ in an angry way when you ask them to be quiet.
6. I don't think they should ________________ people to speak on their phones on buses. It's too noisy.
7. Please ________________ the volume! It's too loud.
8. Answering your cell phone during dinner is very ________________.
9. Can you ________________ this song? It's my favorite!
10. Can you ________________ that cute photo of us from the party on social media? I love it.

C Complete each sentence with a verb in the infinitive or gerund form.

1. I love ________________________________
2. I decided ________________________________
3. I hate ________________________________
4. I dislike ________________________________
5. I want ________________________________
6. I can't stand ________________________________
7. I finished ________________________________
8. I try ________________________________

READING AND WRITING

A Read the article. Match each question from the box to the correct paragraph.

a. Are you being rude?
b. Are you too **attached** to your phone?
c. Are you being unsafe with your phone?
d. Do you use your phone for everything?
e. Are you spending too much?

How connected are you?

1. ____________________

Do you use your phone for work, to talk to friends, or only in case of an **emergency**? Can **colleagues** reach you at all hours of the day? If you leave your phone at home, do you worry about missing out on plans with your friends? You may be addicted to using your phone! Try to spend less time checking your phone. You will feel less stressed.

2. ____________________

Do you go on social media, call and text your friends, look up directions, listen to music, take pictures, and order food and taxis on your phone? Do you talk to your friends more through texts than in person?

3. ____________________

Is the price for these services too expensive? Do your monthly phone charges fit in your **budget**? If you use too much data every month, you usually have to pay more. If this happens to you, you ought to think about finding a new plan or using your phone less.

4. ____________________

You need two hands to drive a car. Taking your hand off the steering wheel to use your phone is **risky**. Even using your phone "hands free" is dangerous because you may not pay enough attention to the road. In some places, it's **illegal** to speak on the phone while driving. If you need to make or receive a call, stop on the side of the road. Do not put yourself or others in danger.

5. ____________________

Turn your phone off in meetings, movie theaters, restaurants, or any place where a ringing phone might **disturb** people. It's OK to use your phone in a public place; just remember to speak softly and keep your conversation **private**.

If you answered yes to most of these questions, you should **reconsider** how you use your phone in your daily life. It's nice to be connected, but you shouldn't let technology **get in the way of** your life.

B Write the bold words from the article that match the definitions below.

1. very serious problem that needs immediate action ____________________
2. against the law ____________________
3. not public ____________________
4. dangerous ____________________
5. annoy ____________________
6. how much money you can spend ____________________
7. coworkers ____________________
8. prevent something from happening or make something more difficult ____________________
9. think about something again ____________________
10. emotionally connected to something ____________________

C Complete the text with the gerund or infinitive form of the verbs in parentheses.

I don't want **(1.** give**)** ____________________ my personal cell phone number to my colleagues. I'm an office manager, and I dislike **(2.** talk**)** ____________________ about work during my free time. I finish **(3.** work**)** ____________________ at 10:00 pm, and I hate **(4.** get**)** ____________________ business calls after that. So, I have decided **(5.** wait**)** ____________________ until the next morning to respond to any late calls. That way I don't need **(6.** answer**)** ____________________ a lot of silly questions late at night. I prefer **(7.** make**)** ____________________ calls in the morning.

D What are the good and bad points about having a cell phone? Complete the chart with your own ideas.

Good points	Bad points

E Do you know anyone who is addicted to their phone? Why do you think so? Write your answers in your notebook.

11

TECHNOLOGY

A THEN AND NOW

VOCABULARY

A Complete the words.

1. w e ___ ___ ___ ___ l e
2. a ___ ___ a ___ c e d
3. r ___ l ___ ___ b ___ ___
4. a f f ___ r ___ ___ ___ ___ ___
5. ___ u s t ___ ___ i ___ a ___ ___ e
6. r e ___ ___ a r ___ e ___ b ___ ___
7. f ___ s h ___ ___ n ___ ___ ___ e
8. u ___ ___ r- ___ r ___ ___ ___ d l y
9. p ___ a ___ t i ___ ___ l
10. d ___ r ___ ___ l ___

B Write the words from **A** next to the correct meaning.

1. can be worn ____________________
2. can be trusted; dependable ____________________
3. not very expensive ____________________
4. stylish; trendy ____________________
5. strong and unlikely to break ____________________
6. has a battery that can be charged again ____________________
7. useful and logical ____________________
8. can be changed to fit your personal needs ____________________
9. easy to use ____________________
10. very modern ____________________

C Complete the sentences with the words from **A** and **B**.

1. My favorite piece of ____________________ technology is my smart watch. I wear it every day.
2. This program is so ____________________. Everyone in my family can use it easily.
3. My phone must be very ____________________ because I've dropped it a lot, and it still works.
4. That is a very ____________________ phone case! I love the pattern on it.
5. She wants to find an ____________________ laptop because she doesn't have a lot of money.
6. We use the most ____________________ software on the market. This program is brand new.
7. This laptop is very ____________________. I've never had a problem with it.
8. The settings are ____________________, so you can easily change them to work for you.

CONVERSATION

A Unscramble the words in order to make sentences. Add commas where necessary.

1. **Other people:** say / some / people / cell phones / dangerous / that / are

   ____

   You: save / in / reality / they / lives / can

   ____

2. **Other people:** a smartphone / should have / some / think / people / that / everyone

   ____

   You: truth / but / it's / the / is / necessary / not

   ____

3. **Other people:** some / say / people / I'm / shy / that

   ____

   You: outgoing / but / I'm / actually / my / with / friends

   ____

4. **Other people:** a lot / people / think / of / like / I / only / hip-hop music

   ____

   You: classical music / but / listen / I / to / too / in fact

   ____

B Complete the sentences with expressions used to offer counterarguments, like those in **A**.

1. Some people say that technology is all bad. ______________, it helps us a lot.
2. Some people think that cell phones are too expensive. ______________ they aren't.
3. ______________________________.
   But, in reality, some people don't need a cell phone.
4. ______________________________.
   But, the truth is, cell phones make life more complicated.

C Write pairs of sentences stating what other people think about something and what you think about it.

1. **Other people:** ______________________________
   You: ______________________________
2. **Other people:** ______________________________
   You: ______________________________
3. **Other people:** ______________________________
   You: ______________________________
4. **Other people:** ______________________________
   You: ______________________________

GRAMMAR

A Write sentences about things you used to do. Use the categories below.

1. fashion: *I used to wear a baseball cap all the time.*
2. fashion: ______
3. music: ______
4. hobbies: ______
5. food: ______
6. TV shows: ______
7. place you lived: ______

B Maria Dominguez used to be a computer programmer. Now she is the president of one of the largest technology companies in the world. Write questions to ask her with *use to*.

1. ______ less money?
2. ______ work?
3. ______ night classes?
4. ______ in an apartment?
5. ______ a lot for tests?
6. ______?

C Mark each sentence correct (C) or incorrect (I). Then rewrite the incorrect sentences.

______ 1. Claudia didn't used to speak English very often.
______ 2. Takashi doesn't drink coffee now, but he used to drink six cups a day.
______ 3. When I was a child, I used to playing outdoors all day in the summer.
______ 4. Did you use to study a lot when you were in high school?
______ 5. We used to take the subway to work, but now we drive.
______ 6. Andrei didn't use to exercise very much.
______ 7. Now, Young-Hee uses to visit her grandparents every Saturday.
______ 8. When you lived in California, did you used to go to the beach often?

D Match the sentences.

______ 1. Family members used to live close to each other.
______ 2. Smartphones didn't use to be affordable.
______ 3. Not many people used to have a computer.
______ 4. People used to walk a lot.
______ 5. Our town didn't use to have any fast food restaurants.

a. Today, a lot of people own one.
b. Now, there are three on Main Street.
c. Now, they aren't as expensive.
d. Nowadays, they live farther apart.
e. These days, many people drive everywhere.

B MAKING LIFE BETTER

VOCABULARY AND GRAMMAR

A Choose the correct answers to complete the sentences.

1. Of course, it isn't working. You need to **load** / **plug in** the TV!
2. Could you **look up** / **switch on** the train schedule online?
3. My alarm **goes off** / **runs out** at 7 am every weekday.
4. **Log in** / **Scroll down** with your username and password.
5. I **loaded** / **switched on** the washing machine with your laundry this morning.
6. You have to **go off** / **stand up** during your presentation so everyone can see you.

B Complete the instructions with the words in the box.

charge	look up	plug in	run out	scroll down	switch on

Dear Grandpa,

Here are some simple instructions on how to use your first smartphone!

- First, (1.) ____________ your charger. Then, connect it to your phone and wait for the phone to (2.) ____________. Make sure you always do this when the battery symbol is near empty. This means your battery will (3.) ____________ soon.
- Second, when it is charged, (4.) ____________ the phone and enter your password.
- Finally, from the home screen, (5.) ____________ to your phone book, (6.) ____________ my number, and call me! (I added the number for you.)

Talk to you soon!

Petra

C Read the description. Then complete the sentences using (*not*) *as . . . as* comparisons. Use contractions when possible.

Franklin and Gino are best friends. Gino is a good soccer player. However, he can't play basketball very well. He's 5′8″. Franklin is a great basketball player, and he's 6′5″. But, he isn't so good at soccer. Both men are 25 years old. Gino is very outgoing and has a lot of friends. Franklin is a very shy person and only has a small group of close friends.

1. Gino (be, tall) ____________ Franklin.
2. Gino (play, well) ____________ basketball ____________ Franklin.
3. Franklin (play, well) ____________ soccer ____________ Gino.
4. Gino (be, old) ____________ Franklin.
5. Franklin (have, many friends) ____________ Gino.
6. Gino (be, shy) ____________ Franklin.

READING AND WRITING

A Scan the article quickly. Write the appliances the article mentions on the line below.

___

Technology Report — June 9

In today's report, we look at a new trend in technology called the *internet of things*.

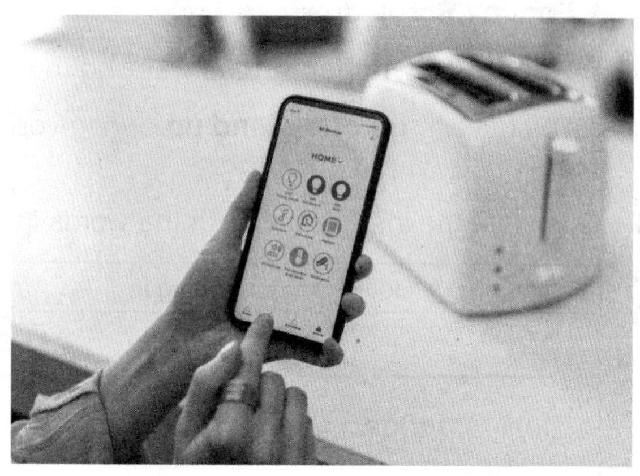

The internet of things means putting tiny computers into everyday electronic appliances, such as toasters and microwaves. With this new technology, appliances can communicate with their users—and with other appliances!

Many companies now sell products that are part of the internet of things, like a smart toaster. It remembers your favorite kind of toast: light or dark. Companies have also designed a smart coffee maker. Not only can it measure water and coffee, but it can also remember to put milk in your coffee at breakfast and make black coffee in the afternoon. In addition, there's a smart alarm clock that can show you the weather, play music, and even communicate with other devices and give you information. For example, it can tell you, "Your coffee maker needs more water."

And that's only the beginning. Now, it's possible to have a smart home, in which the lights, heater, and air conditioner change automatically when family members come home. This makes the home comfortable, and it saves a lot of energy. The internet of things could change many parts of our daily lives.

But do people really want this? Do they really need technology everywhere? One company asked people about their opinions on smart appliances. Some answers were surprising. A smart refrigerator can buy more food online, but people didn't want that because the refrigerator could make mistakes.

Some people say that smart technology will someday be as important as the telephone. But, in fact, many of these products are not useful, or even practical. Companies should learn more about the technology that people really want.

B Read the article again. Circle **T** for *true* or **F** for *false*.

1. A smart toaster has a computer inside. **T F**
2. People can buy products like this now. **T F**
3. Smart houses use more energy. **T F**
4. A smart alarm clock can communicate with other devices. **T F**
5. The people that one company spoke to wanted a smart refrigerator. **T F**
6. The writer of the report believes all smart technology is useful. **T F**

C Match each word from the report with the correct meaning.

_____ 1. appliances a. create a plan to make something

_____ 2. communicate b. send messages

_____ 3. design c. machines for the home

_____ 4. technology d. science used to invent useful things

D Use the words in **C** to complete the sentences.

1. Cell phones help us ____________________ with each other.
2. Without modern ____________________, we wouldn't have cell phones and computers.
3. Scientists ____________________ some amazing things.
4. My favorite ____________________ are my vacuum cleaner and my washing machine.

E Write about your favorite way to communicate. Compare it with other ways.

12

TRAVEL

A BEFORE YOU GO

VOCABULARY

A Complete the travel checklist with the words from the box.

apply for	book	check in	download	exchange	get	lock	pack	valid	water

1. check that passport is still ________________
2. ________________ a visa
3. ________________ plane tickets
4. ________________ travel insurance
5. ________________ some money
6. ________________ a weather app and check weather in Copenhagen
7. ________________ suitcase (remember travel adapter!)
8. ask Zara to ________________ the plants
9. ________________ for the flight online
10. ________________ the front door

B Complete the sentences with phrases from **A**. Use the correct verb form.

1. Have you ________________ your train ________________ yet?
2. You may need to ________________ for a ________________ if you want to travel to Ghana.
3. It's important to buy ________________ in case you get into an accident or lose your luggage.
4. Sami always ________________ instead of waiting in line at the airport.
5. I downloaded ________________ yesterday so I can check for rain before leaving the hotel.
6. Make sure you ________________ because the plugs in the UK are different.
7. I hope she remembered to ________________. I don't want them to die!
8. Should we ________________ some ________________ at the airport? We need cash for a taxi.
9. Check the date on your passport to make sure it is ________________.
10. Make sure you ________________ when you leave the house!

C Look at the travel checklist in **A** again. Do you usually do these things to prepare for a trip? Why or why not? Write your answers in your notebook.

CONVERSATION

A Match the sentence halves.

_____ 1. I forgot	a. I put the house keys.
_____ 2. I forgot to	b. locking the door.
_____ 3. I don't remember	c. water the plants.
_____ 4. I can't remember where	d. my passport.

B Complete the conversations by writing sentences that say what the people forgot. Use expressions from **A** (*I forgot*, *I forgot to*, *I don't remember*, *I can't remember where*).

1. **A:** *I forgot my umbrella.*
   B: Maybe you can buy an umbrella in the department store.
2. **A:** ______________________________
   B: I saw your credit card on the desk.
3. **A:** ______________________________
   B: That's OK. I have a jacket you can borrow.
4. **A:** ______________________________
   B: You can use my English textbook. I don't need it now.
5. **A:** ______________________________
   B: I think your keys are in the kitchen.
6. **A:** ______________________________
   B: No problem. There's a lot of food in the refrigerator.
7. **A:** ______________________________
   B: You paid that bill yesterday!

C Write your own conversation with a friend who often forgets things.

Your friend: ______________________________
You: ______________________________
Your friend: ______________________________
You: ______________________________
Your friend: ______________________________
You: ______________________________
Your friend: ______________________________
You: ______________________________
Your friend: ______________________________
You: ______________________________

GRAMMAR

A Read what students have to do before studying at a university in the United States. Then fill in the answers for your country.

	US	Your country
1. get good grades in high school	yes	
2. pass an entrance exam	no	
3. fill out a lot of forms	yes	
4. get letters from their teachers	yes (usually)	
5. visit the university	no	

B Write a sentence for each of the ten answers in **A**. Use *have to / don't have to*, *must*, and *have got to.*

1. In the US, students ______________________ good grades in high school.
2. They ______________________
3. ______________________
4. ______________________
5. ______________________
6. In ______________, students ______________________
7. They ______________________
8. ______________________
9. ______________________
10. ______________________

C Write true sentences about yourself.

What did you have to do yesterday?

1. Yesterday, I ______________________

____

2. I also ______________________

____

What do you have to do every day at work or school?

3. Every day, I ______________________

____

4. I ______________________

____

B ADVENTURES IN TRAVELING

VOCABULARY AND GRAMMAR

A Complete the chart with the words from the box.

boarding	bus stop	catch	delayed	depart	gate	itinerary	schedule	take off	terminal

Information with times and dates	Places to take transportation	Verbs	Transportation status

B Write words from **A** next to their opposites.

1. ______________ ↔ arrive
2. ______________ ↔ on time
3. ______________ ↔ land
4. ______________ ↔ miss
5. ______________ ↔ getting off

C Write questions to match the answers.

***Yes / No* questions**

1. **Simple present:** ______________________________?
   Yes, they drive to work every day.
2. **Present continuous:** ______________________________?
   Yes, I'm shopping right now.
3. **Present perfect:** ______________________________?
   No, I've never been to Peru, but I want to go.
4. **Simple past:** ______________________________?
   Yes, I did. I visited Grandma yesterday.
5. **Modal verbs (can, should, etc.):** ______________________________?
   Yes, certainly. I can send you the documents today.

***Wh-* questions**

1. **Simple present:** ______________________________?
   I usually eat sushi for lunch.
2. **Present continuous:** ______________________________?
   I'm thinking of going to Malaysia on my next vacation.
3. **Present perfect:** ______________________________?
   I've been to a yoga class once.
4. **Simple past:** ______________________________?
   I applied for my visa last week.
5. **Future with *will*:** ______________________________?
   I'll be in Bogota until March.

READING AND WRITING

A Read the article. Fill in the blanks with the subheadings from the box.

Other ideas	Pre-trip planning	Saving space	Tagging luggage	Your carry-on bag

Tips for Better Packing

Whether you are planning to travel for a weekend or several months, around the country or overseas, here are some tips to help you pack your bags.

❶ ____________________

- You need a packing list to help you remember everything. Make your list and **review** it about a week before your trip.
- Plan a time to go shopping for things you need for your trip.
- Don't pack the night before you travel. You will forget things because you're **hurrying**.

❷ ____________________

- Before packing, put name **tags** on **valuable** items like cameras and cell phones.
- Make sure that each piece of luggage, including carry-ons, has a tag on it.
- If you know your hotel's address and phone number, put it on the tags.

❸ ____________________

- Pack small items (socks, belts, etc.) inside your shoes. It uses the empty space and helps the shoes hold their shape.
- If you are traveling with a friend, plan your packing together. Share your shampoo, toothpaste, or **first-aid kit**.

❹ ____________________

- The most important items for your trip (passport, plane tickets, credit cards, keys, etc.) should go in your carry-on bag. Always keep them with you.
- Keep your carry-on bag small and light. Put **bulky**, heavy items in your checked luggage.
- Use soft bags, such as backpacks or shoulder bags, for carry-ons. They fit easily under the airplane seat, or into small overhead compartments.

❺ ____________________

- Bring an empty bag for souvenirs from the trip.
- Remember to pack **a few** rubber bands, safety pins, and plastic bags. They can be very useful.
- Bring some snacks, such as nuts, cookies, or dried fruit (not chocolate—it's too messy). You can eat them if you don't have time for a meal.

B According to the article, are these good ideas or bad ideas? Check (✓) the correct column.

	Good idea	Bad idea
1. Put your credit cards in your checked luggage.		
2. Bring chocolate as a snack.		
3. Make a list before you start packing.		
4. Share shampoo with a friend.		
5. Pack a few hours before your trip.		
6. Go shopping before your trip.		
7. Put large things in your carry-on bag.		

C Write the words in bold from the article in **A** next to the correct meanings.

1. ____________________ going fast
2. ____________________ labels
3. ____________________ about three
4. ____________________ worth a lot of money or important to someone
5. ____________________ check that something is correct
6. ____________________ a set of medical supplies
7. ____________________ takes up too much space

D Read the interview and circle the correct answers.

A: So, tell me about your travel experiences. (1.) **Have you traveled** / **Did you travel** to many different cities in the US?

B: Yes, I've been to Miami, San Francisco, and New York, but the most interesting city (2.) **I've ever visited** / **I'm ever visiting** is Washington, DC.

A: Really? When (3.) **can you go** / **did you go** there?

B: I went last year with some friends. You should definitely go sometime!

A: Tell me more. Why (4.) **will I** / **should I** travel to Washington, DC?

B: Well, you (5.) **don't have to** / **must not** bring a lot of money for tourist attractions. Many of the museums, such as the National Air and Space Museum, are free.

A: That's great! What (6.) **will be** / **was** your favorite part of the trip?

B: My favorite part was the National Zoo. We saw a lot of amazing animals and (7.) **are taking** / **took** some great photos.

A: It sounds like a wonderful trip. (8.) **Will you go** / **Have you gone** back someday?

B: Yes! In fact, I'll probably go back this spring.

E Imagine someone is interviewing you about your travel experiences or your travel plans for the future. Write the interview questions and your answers below.

Interviewer: ______________________________

You: ______________________________

Interviewer: ______________________________

You: ______________________________

Interviewer: ______________________________

You: ______________________________

Interviewer: ______________________________

You: ______________________________

Interviewer: ______________________________

You: ______________________________